Library Learning Information

To renew this item call:

0115 929 3388

or visit

www.ideastore.co.uk

TOWER HAMLETS

Created and managed by Tower Hamlets Council

Light

Written by Sally Hewitt

W

FRANKLIN WATTS
LONDON•SYDNEY

First published as *Starting Science: Light* in 2009 by
Franklin Watts. This edition 2013
338 Euston Road, London NW1 3BH

Franklin Watts Australia
Level 17/207 Kent Street, Sydney NSW 2000

Editor: Katie Dicker
Art Direction: Dibakar Acharjee (Q2AMedia)
Designer: Neha Kaul (Q2AMedia)
Picture researcher: Kamal Kumar (Q2AMedia)
Craft models made by: Tarang Saggar (Q2AMedia)
Photography: Dibakar Acharjee (Q2AMedia)

Picture credits:
t=top b=bottom c=centre l=left r=right

Cover: Iakov Kalinin/Shutterstock.
Title page: Antinolo Jorge Sierra/Photolibrary.
Insides: Tero Niemi/Jupiter Images: 6, Rob
Melnychuk/Alamy: 7t, Richard Sargeant/Shutterstock: 7b,
Antinolo Jorge Sierra/Photolibrary: 8t, Nasa: 8b, Dejan
Suc/Istockphoto: 10t, Joe Mercier/Shutterstock: 10b,
Ekaterina Krasnikova/Shutterstock: 12, Thomas
Northcut/Riser/Getty Images: 14, Photostogo,
Udoudo/Dreamstime, Elnur/Shutterstock: 15tr, Roman
Sigaev/Shutterstock: 16t, SW Productions/Photolibrary:
16b, Jan van der Hoeven/Shutterstock: 18, Donald
Miralle/Stringer/Getty Images: 19tr, Polka Dot
Images/Jupiter Images: 20bl, Anetta/Shutterstock: 20br,
Martin Fischer/Shutterstock: 22, Paul Ridsdale/Alamy:
23tr, Olegmit/Dreamstime: 24, Monika
Gniot/Shutterstock: 25tr, Samantha Roche/Fotolia: 26,
Ljupco Smokovski/Shutterstock: 27tr.
Q2AMedia Image Bank: Imprint page, Contents page,
9, 11, 13, 15, 17, 19, 21, 23, 25, 27.
Q2AMedia Art Bank: 20, 24.

With thanks to our models Harleen Mehta, Shruti
Aggarwal and Tarang Saggar.

Every attempt has been made to clear copyright.
Should there be any inadvertent omission, please
apply to the publisher for rectification.

A CIP catalogue record for this book
is available from the British Library

ISBN: 978 1 4451 1918 2

Dewey Classification: 535.'22

Printed in China

Franklin Watts is a division of Hachette Children's
Books, an Hachette UK company.
www.hachette.co.uk

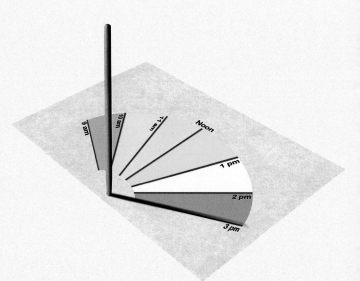

Contents

What is light?   6

What is dark?   8

Light rays   10

Shadows   12

Shining through   14

Reflection   16

Refraction   18

Bigger and smaller   20

Different kinds of light   22

Seeing and light   24

Coloured light   26

Glossary   28

Index   30

Words that appear in **bold** can be found in the glossary on pages 28–29.

What is light?

Light is a kind of **energy**. The Sun is the greatest source of light on Earth. Our eyes need light to see, so when the Sun goes down at night, we turn on lights or burn candles to see.

The Sun gives out the heat and light energy that all life on Earth needs to survive.

Travelling light

Light travels in a straight line at 300,000 kilometres a second. It is the fastest moving thing in the universe! Light from the Sun takes about 8 minutes 20 seconds to travel through space to Earth. You must never look directly at the Sun. It is too bright for our eyes.

Luminous

Things that give out light are **luminous**. Some luminous things give out brighter, more intense light than others. The brightness of car headlights is more intense than the brightness of candlelight, for example.

This torch is luminous. It gives out a beam of light to read by.

Reflected light

We see some objects when light bounces off them, or is **reflected** into our eyes. The Moon is not luminous so it does not give out light. We see the Moon when the Sun shines on it. The Moon reflects sunlight into our eyes.

Moonlight is pale because it is reflected light from the Sun.

What is dark?

Where there is no light, it is dark. It is dark wherever light cannot reach – in your bedroom when you turn out the light and close the curtains, at the bottom of the sea and in deep caves, for example.

Living in the dark

Some animals, such as owls, have large eyes to help them see in the dark. Other animals use their senses of smell and touch in the darkness. Some deep-sea fish and night insects make their own light and glow in the dark to attract prey or find a mate.

Glow-worms give out a green glow or a flashing light to attract a mate in the dark.

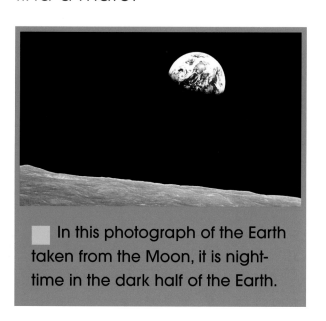

In this photograph of the Earth taken from the Moon, it is night-time in the dark half of the Earth.

Day and night

Earth takes 24 hours to spin around once in space. It is night when the half of Earth you are on is turning away from the Sun. It is day when your half of Earth is facing the Sun.

Make a model Earth

Ask an adult to help you with this activity

You will need:
- bowl and spoon • water
- flour • salt • scales
- round balloon • newspaper
- straight stick about 50 cm long • pen and paints
- atlas • torch

1 In a bowl, stir 375 ml of water, 75 grams of flour and 7 grams of salt together to make a smooth paste like glue.

2 Blow up the balloon and tie the end securely. Tear strips of newspaper about 6 cm by 3 cm and dip them into the paste. Stick the strips onto the balloon in layers to make a round

ball-shaped 'Earth'. Leave to dry. When the paper is dry, ask an adult to help you pop the balloon and push the stick carefully through the centre of the ball and out the other side.

3 Paint the ball to look like Earth, with the stick going through the north and south pole. Use an atlas to find where you are on Earth and mark this position on your planet.

4 In a darkened room, hold your model Earth in a beam of torchlight. Gradually turn the stick and watch your part of Earth move from day to night.

Light rays

Light travels away from a light source in straight lines called rays. Sometimes you can see rays of light from the Sun shining through trees, from behind clouds or through a window.

Lighting up the dark

Rays from a strong light source, such as the Sun, travel long distances and light up a large area. Rays from a weaker source, such as a candle, travel shorter distances and light up a small area.

Rays of sunlight are shining through gaps between the trees in this forest.

A lighthouse sweeps a powerful beam of light across the water to warn ships of danger.

One direction

Light can only travel in straight lines (or beams). You can clearly see the straight, narrow beam of a torch or car headlight in the dark, for example. A theatre spotlight sends out a beam of light to show a dancer on the stage, leaving the rest of the theatre in darkness.

Hit the target!

Ask an adult to help you with this activity

You will need:
- 1 square of paper and 5 squares of strong card (15 cm x 15 cm)
- scissors • pencil and paints (or coloured pens)
- modelling clay • ruler • torch

1 Fold the paper in half both ways to find the centre point. Open it out and put it on top of four of the card squares.

2 Ask an adult to push sharp scissors through the centre of the four pieces of card, using the paper as a guide. Cut a small circle around each hole. Leave the fifth card uncut – this will be

your target. Draw a target around the centre.

3 Push each piece of card into a ball of modelling clay (for a stand). Line them up on a table or on the floor about 20 cm apart, with the target at one end of the line. Shine the torch beam through the hole at the other end of the line. Can you line up the holes so the beam of light shines through them and hits the target?

Shadows

Light cannot go around corners. When something solid gets in the way of light rays, light cannot shine through it or go around it. This creates a **shadow** the same shape as the solid object.

You are solid. When you make a shape, your shadow makes the same shape as you.

Different shadows

As the Earth turns around, the Sun seems to move across the sky. In the morning and evening, when the Sun is low in the sky, your shadow is longer than you are. At midday, when the Sun is overhead, your shadow is shorter.

Make a sundial

Ask an adult to help you with this activity

You will need:
- Strong, thick A3 card • length of dowel (thin rod of wood), about 25 cm • sticky tape or glue • compass • ruler
- waterproof marker pen
- waterproof paints

1 Ask an adult to make a hole in the card, half-way down one of the long sides, about 2 cm from the edge.

2 Push the dowel into the hole so the base of the dowel is level with the underside of the card. Tape or glue it in place so it stands upright. Alternatively, place the sundial on some grass and push the dowel through the hole into the grass to secure it.

3 Use a compass to place the sundial so the stick edge of the card is facing south.

Stick edge

4 On a sunny day, on every hour, with your ruler and marker pen draw a line along the shadow made by the stick. Write the time on each line – 9.00, 10.00, 11.00, etc., and paint each segment.

5 Put your sundial in the same place to tell the time on sunny days. The shadow will move throughout the day as the position of the Sun changes.

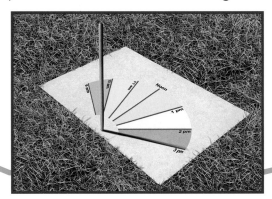

Shining through

Light can shine through **transparent materials**. Glass, clear plastic and water are transparent – you can see through them. Light cannot shine through **opaque** materials such as wood, metal and card.

Translucent

Some materials are **translucent**, which means some light can pass through them. Sunglasses are translucent. They help to protect your eyes from harmful Sun rays. Tracing paper and tissue paper are both translucent materials. When you look through them you can see some light, but only blurred shapes.

Net curtains are translucent. They cover a window, but allow some light to pass through them.

Materials

Materials are often chosen because of the way light shines through them. Glass, for example, is transparent. Glass windows let you see in and out. Thick bedroom curtains are opaque. They keep out the light to help you sleep.

You can clearly see how much water is in a glass beaker (left). Plastic beakers let less light through them.

Make a light and shadows collage

You will need:
- selection of paper (e.g. white paper, coloured tissue paper, tracing paper)
- foil • thin card • thin white cotton material • scissors
- sheet of clear plastic (A3)
- glue • powerful torch

1 Cut different shapes from the paper, foil, card and cotton. Stick them onto one side of the clear plastic sheet to make a picture.

2 Try to guess which materials will let light through. Make a chart to show your guesses.

3 In a dark room, shine the torch through the plastic sheet onto a white wall. How good were your guesses? What do you notice about the shadows?

Reflection

When rays of light hit something, they bounce off it, like a ball bouncing off a hard surface. This is called reflection. Different surfaces cause the light rays to reflect in different ways.

Smooth and rough

When light hits a smooth surface, such as flat water in a pond, it bounces off in one direction and you see a reflection. Light bounces off rough, uneven surfaces in all directions. You don't see a clear reflection in a choppy sea, for example.

Light bounces off ripples on the surface of the sea and creates sparkles.

Mirrors

Mirrors are made of smooth glass covering a layer of shiny metal. When light rays hit the mirror, they bounce straight back and you see your reflection.

You can see your reflection in a flat, shiny mirror.

16

Make a kaleidoscope

You will need:
- 3 rectangles of foil card, all the same size (about 20 cm x 5 cm) or very shiny foil glued onto card
- sticky tape • pencil
- white paper • scissors
- coloured paper shapes or metallic confetti
- plastic food wrap

1 Tape the foil card rectangles together to make a triangular **prism** with the shiny side facing inwards.

2 Draw around the triangular end onto the white paper and cut out the triangle shape. Stick the paper triangle to one end of the prism. Drop the coloured paper shapes (or confetti)

into the prism and seal the open end of your kaleidoscope with plastic food wrap.

3 Hold your kaleidoscope up to the light and look through the plastic wrap. You will see a repeated pattern of coloured shapes. Shake the kaleidoscope to change the pattern.

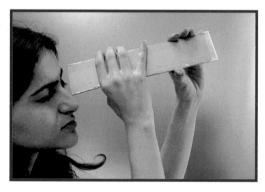

Light from the coloured shapes bounces from mirror to mirror and you see several reflections that make repeated patterns.

Refraction

Light travels through water and glass more slowly than it travels through air. When light passes from glass or water to the surrounding air, the rays slightly change direction and bend. This is called **refraction**.

Bending light

Refraction makes straight objects, such as a pencil or a canoe paddle, look bent when they are half in and half out of water. This is because light changes direction as it moves from water to air.

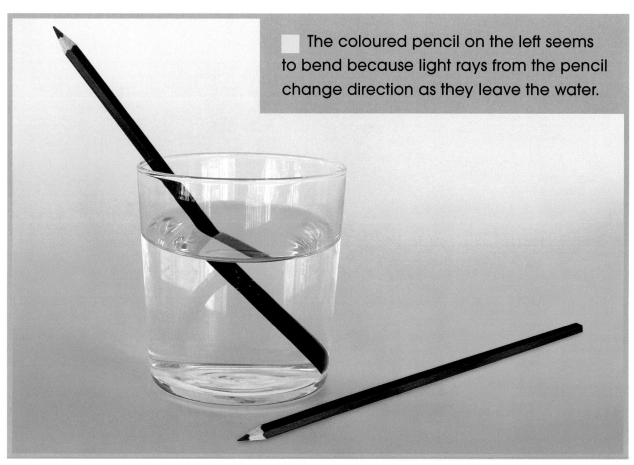

The coloured pencil on the left seems to bend because light rays from the pencil change direction as they leave the water.

Bending shapes

If you look through a big raindrop on a windowpane, the objects you see through the glass will appear to have strange shapes. This is because rays of light bend as they travel through the glass and the water, and change the shape of the things you see.

You see distorted shapes through the raindrops on a window because the light rays are refracted.

Use refraction for a magic trick!

You will need:
• bowl • coin • modelling clay • jug of water

1 Place the bowl on a table. Fix a coin to the bottom far side of the bowl with modelling clay.

2 Ask a friend to look at the coin and then move slowly backwards and stop when the coin disappears from view.

3 Pour some water into the bowl. Your friend will be amazed to see the coin reappear!

Light reflected from the coin is bent as it leaves the water and goes into the air, helping your friend to see the coin again.

Bigger and smaller

Lenses are pieces of curved glass or other transparent material, such as plastic. They refract light rays shining through them and cause them to change direction.

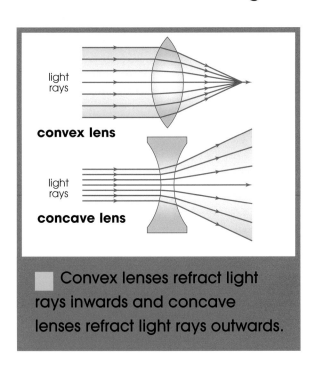

light rays

convex lens

light rays

concave lens

Convex lenses refract light rays inwards and concave lenses refract light rays outwards.

Concave and convex

Lenses in glasses help to focus images onto the back of our eyes (see page 25). **Convex lenses** help long-sighted people who cannot see near things clearly. **Concave lenses** help short-sighted people who cannot see distant things well.

Microscope

A **microscope** uses convex lenses to make tiny things look thousands of times bigger than they really are. Light is reflected off a mirror onto the **sample** and through a series of lenses to reach our eyes.

Leaf veins

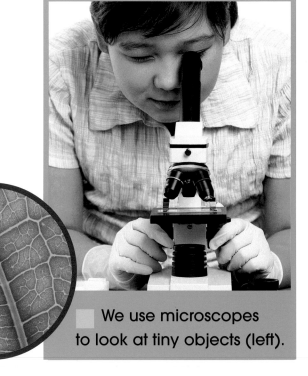

We use microscopes to look at tiny objects (left).

20

Make a microscope

Ask an adult to help you with this activity

You will need:
- clear plastic bottle • scissors
- small mirror • modelling clay
- cup of water • human hair

1 Ask an adult to help you cut the top off the bottle. Then cut two narrow vertical strips out of opposite sides of the bottle, and two short horizontal slits near the top of the bottle in the other two sides (see the template below).

2 strips cut from bottle sides

Template

horizontal slit

2 Angle the small mirror in the bottom of the bottle to reflect light upwards. Use the modelling clay as a support. Push each end of one of the vertical strips into the small horizontal slits to make a platform.

3 Drip one drop of water onto the platform to form a convex lens. Use the other strip as a slide. Put a hair onto the strip and hold it under the platform. The hair will be magnified by the water drop.

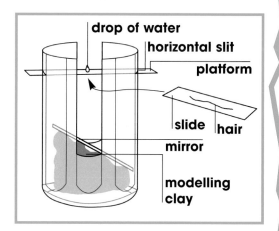

drop of water
horizontal slit
platform
slide | hair
mirror
modelling clay

You can use a magnifying glass to make it look even bigger!

Different kinds of light

Luminous objects glow in different ways. **Incandescent light** is given out by heat. The Sun gives out incandescent light. When **electricity** passes through older light bulbs, the wire becomes red hot and glows with incandescent light.

Light in nature

Lightning is a type of natural incandescent light that you see in a storm. During a storm, natural electricity builds up in a cloud and creates a huge spark that we see as a flash of lighting and hear as a crash of thunder.

A flash of lightning lights up the night sky for a few seconds and then disappears.

Fluorescence

Things that are **fluorescent** do not glow by themselves. They glow in the dark, for example, when light shines on them. Fluorescent strips on clothes glow in the dark when they are caught in the headlights of a car or truck.

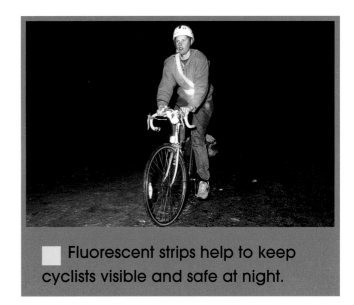

Fluorescent strips help to keep cyclists visible and safe at night.

Make a glow in the dark mobile

Ask an adult to help you with this activity

You will need:
- different coloured fluorescent card
- pencil • scissors • glue
- hole puncher • string
- coat hanger • torch

1 Fold the cards in half and draw on night-time shapes such as ghosts, stars, moons and owls. Cut the shapes out of the double card.

2 Stick the shapes together so both sides are fluorescent. Punch a hole near the top of each shape and attach different lengths of string.

3 Tie your night-time shapes onto the coat hanger and hang it in your bedroom.

4 Test how your mobile glows best – in a completely dark room, in torchlight or in daylight.

Seeing and light

We see things around us when light reflects off them into our eyes. It's difficult to see at night when there is only a little light. We see nothing at all in total darkness.

Letting in light

The black circle in the middle of our eyes, called the **pupil**, is a hole that lets in light. The **iris** controls how much light enters our eyes by making the pupil bigger or smaller. This helps our eyes to cope with different strengths of light.

This diagram shows some of the different parts of our eyes.

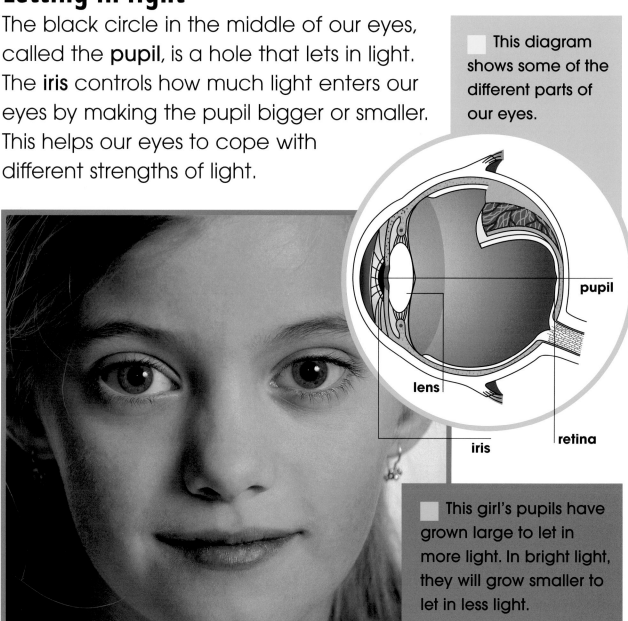

pupil

lens

iris

retina

This girl's pupils have grown large to let in more light. In bright light, they will grow smaller to let in less light.

Lenses

Inside our eyes, behind the pupil, is a lens. Reflected light from an object, such as a flower, shines through the pupil onto the lens. The lens focuses this light onto the **retina** and makes an upside-down image of the flower. Our brain turns the image around so we see the flower the right way up.

Light is reflected from these flowers into our eyes, so we can see them.

Make a camera

Ask an adult to help you with this activity

You will need:
- small square box without a lid (such as a gift box) • tracing paper • sticky tape • lamp
- magnifying glass

1 Stretch the tracing paper tightly over the open end of the box and tape it in place to make a smooth screen.

2 Ask an adult to make a pinhole in the middle of the opposite side of the box. In a darkened room, point the pinhole at a bright object such as a lamp.

3 Hold the magnifying glass to act as a lens between the lamp

and the pinhole. You will see the lamp reflected upside down onto the screen.

Your camera shows how our eyes work. Light enters the small hole (pupil) and shines onto the tracing paper (retina).

Coloured light

Light around us seems to be white but, in fact, it is made up of different colours. We only see these colours when light is refracted through something transparent, such as a glass prism.

The spectrum

The colours that make up light are called the **spectrum**. When light shines through a glass prism, the colours travel at different speeds and bend a slightly different amount. The colours separate and we see red, orange, yellow, green, light blue, dark blue and purple.

When sunlight shines through raindrops, they act as tiny prisms and separate the colours of light so we see a rainbow in the sky.

Seeing colours

Our eyes see red, blue and green light. We see the colours of a rainbow when these three colours mix and blend together. A filter is a piece of coloured translucent material, such as glass or tissue paper. A filter only lets light of the same colour through.

We see the different colours of these balloons when mixtures of red, blue and green light are reflected from them.

Mix the colours of light

You will need:
- rectangles of card (70 cm long x 20 cm wide) to make 3 long tubes • sticky tape
- 3 torches • red, blue and green tissue paper (or cellophane) • large sheet of white paper

1 Roll each piece of card lengthwise to make tubes that will fit snugly round the ends of the torches. Tape the long edges together.

2 Tape a tube to the end of each torch and tape a piece of coloured tissue paper over the end of each tube.

3 In a dark room, shine the torches onto the white paper and experiment by mixing the three colours of light.

What different colours can you make?

Glossary

concave lenses
Concave lenses are curved inwards in the middle. They refract light rays outwards.

convex lenses
Convex lenses are curved outwards in the middle. They refract light rays inwards.

electricity
Electricity is a type of energy. We use it to power lights and machines.

energy
Energy is the power that makes things work.

fluorescent
Things that are fluorescent glow in the dark when light shines on them.

incandescent light
Hot objects give out incandescent light. The light from a fire is incandescent.

iris
Your iris is the part of your eye that makes your pupil bigger or smaller to let more or less light through.

lens
A lens is a curved piece of glass or other transparent material that causes light rays to change direction.

luminous
Things that give out light are luminous. The Sun, a torch and a candle are all luminous.

materials
Materials are what things are made of. For example, a book is made of paper and a jumper is made of wool.

microscope
A microscope is a piece of equipment that uses lenses to make tiny objects look bigger.

opaque

You cannot see through things that are opaque and light cannot shine through them.

prism

A prism is a solid shape with three flat sides.

pupil

Your pupil is the black circle in the centre of your eye. It is the opening that lets light into your eye.

reflected

When light is reflected, it bounces off a surface.

refraction

Refraction is the slight bend in light rays when they pass between air and other transparent materials.

retina

The retina is at the back of your eye. It receives images from the lens and sends them to your brain.

sample

A sample is a small part of something used in a test. A sample of hair can be looked at under a microscope, for example.

shadow

A shadow is a patch of darkness made when a solid object blocks light rays.

spectrum

The spectrum is all the colours of light. We see the spectrum when sunlight shines through raindrops and a rainbow appears in the sky.

translucent

Translucent materials only let some light shine through them. We cannot see clearly through translucent materials.

transparent

Light shines through transparent materials such as glass. We can see through them clearly.

Index

air 18, 19
animals 8

candle 6, 7, 10
colour 26, 27

darkness 8, 10, 24
day 8, 9, 12, 13

Earth 6, 8, 9, 12
electricity 22, 28
energy 6, 28
eyes 6, 7, 8, 14, 20, 24, 25, 27

filter 27
fluorescence 23, 28

glass 14, 15, 16, 18, 19, 20,
    26, 27

incandescent light 22, 28

lenses 20, 25, 28
light bulb 22
light rays 10, 12, 16, 18, 19,
    20, 24

lightning 22
luminous 7, 22, 28

materials 14, 15, 20, 27, 28
microscope 20, 21, 28
mirror 16, 17, 20, 21
Moon 7, 8

opaque 14, 15, 29

rainbow 26, 27
reflection 7, 16, 17, 20, 24,
    25, 27, 29
refraction 18, 19, 20, 26, 29

shadow 12, 13, 15, 29
source 6, 10
spectrum 26, 29
Sun 6, 7, 8, 10, 12, 13, 14,
    22, 26

torch 7, 9, 10, 11, 15, 27
translucent 14, 27, 29
transparent 14, 15, 20, 26, 29

water 10, 14, 15, 16, 18, 19, 21